Table of contents

INTRODUCTION

As a dog owner, you want to be the master of your pet but before you can do this, you need to properly train you dog so he can easily cope with the housebreaking rules while adjusting to being a new member of the family.

This eBook, *"**Mastering the Basics of Dog Training for Effective Pet Handling**"* will teach you the fundamentals of Dog Training while enhancing your inherent skills for a more effective bonded relationship between you and your pet.

This book is divided into 3 Major Phases:

- Phase I: Getting Started With Basics for a Strong Foundation
- Phase II: Application Methods for Success
- Phase III: Love and Consistency Over Time

Successful dog training will be beneficial to you and will ensure safety to your household.

I – Phase One

Getting Started With Basics for a Strong Foundation

Building a Relationship with Your Dog: The Number One Strategy of a Dog Whisperer

Bringing home a new dog is not that easy. For you to develop a strong bond based on mutual understanding, you need to do some research on dog breeds before bringing one home. Choose a breed that suits your lifestyle for you to be an effective master and leader.

If you choose a more active breed such as hunting and herding breeds, they require more exercise to stay physically and mentally content. Be sure to assess the dog's energy level before bringing him home.

Dogs in their natural habitat live in packs. It means they look upon someone to lead them for they are naturally submissive. Adult dogs look upon their leader to create that sense of stability. They never question his leadership and the leader in return does not need their affirmation for his position. This creates a natural balance and stability in a pack.

In the dog world, there are only two positions: the leader and the follower.

A pups' first leader is his mother who teaches him all rules, limitations, and boundaries from the first day! Being both a mother and a leader, she evokes a balance of discipline and care which creates a strong bond between them.

To a dog, a leader is someone whom they can trust and follow. A dog can be a loyal friend and follower once they recognize that you are now the leader of their pack.

A dog, even while they are out of their natural habitat, is a social creature that is highly adapted to understanding even your most subtle gestures. If you are training your dog, you need to provide him with the same subtle-assertive leadership that they would experience in a pack.

It is therefore, important that you develop a strong bond between you and your dog without compromising your role as a leader. To do this, you need to show your new dog that you are the "pack leader "from the very first day. Knowing that it takes time, patience, and acceptance, you need to formulate a plan, set your objectives, and follow through if you are to create a strong relationship.

As a pack leader, here are some important points that you need to remember:

Learn Canine Behavior

It is important that you fully understand how a dog behaves depending on the type of breed. Learning more about their body language, gestures, attitude, facial expression and overall behavior is important. Make a thorough research on the breed that you will be bringing home. You must learn to identify the signs that show when your dog is anxious or scared. This will be easier for you to protect your dog or give him assistance if you can understand his movements. Whisperers have a deeper understanding of a dog's language beyond the sounds it emits.

If your dog can trust you with understanding his needs, this will strengthen your bond.

Enlist Your Family in the Training

While in the process of bringing a new dog to your home, make sure to involve the whole family in the training. Let everyone know their specific responsibilities before the new dog arrives. The new dog will become a new member of the family and therefore, needs a proper welcome. This will make the adjustment easier for the new dog if his new pack learns this leadership pack lesson ahead of him.

Train Your Dog

Train your dog as soon as he arrives to assert your leadership over him though you need not put him under stress. Show your dog that a well-trained dog gets more freedom. If he comes when he's called, he can have time without his leash. If they don't go for food on the table, they can be allowed to stay nearby during meals. Training develops his sense of sensitivity and alertness.

Provide a Clear Signal for Communication

Confusions and misunderstandings are often results of disrupted communication, so while you are still in the early phase of training, communicate clearly with your dog. Dogs tend to learn quickly with visual signs than vocal cues, use the former most often and whenever possible.

Paying attention to what you do is your dog's priority rather than paying attention to what you are saying. Since a dog can understand even your subtlest gesture, you don't need to shout at the top of your voice when you're training your dog. You will feel closer with your dog once you learn constant communication with him.

Remain Calm

Shouting or losing your temper over your dog's behavior upsets everyone within the vicinity. Your subtle gestures that exude heat from your blazing temper are enough to notify your pet that his action had displeased you. Regardless of the circumstances, try to give off a sense of calm and tranquility so your dog can count on you to keep cool.

Touch Your Dog As Often As You Can

Researchers believe that physical contact plays a role in enhancing the bond between people and dogs. There is strong evidence that physical contacts like petting and grooming can lessen the stress in sheltered dogs. Remember that a leashed pet is constantly under stress and the only way to calm him down is to give him reassurance that he is safe and comforted through your gentle touch.

Spend Time with Your Dog

Spend time with your dog you can play together, walk together, and stay together. Little moments count in developing a deeper friendship and mutual understanding. Playing games with your dog strengthens the bond.

Create a Schedule to Include a Power-Walk

Out in the wild, while dogs look for their food and water, they explore the world by walking. This activity is deeply ingrained within a dog's natural DNA. Power walking exercises your dog's body as well as stimulates his mind. So include a daily 30-45 minute of power walking to boost your dog's health, both physically and mentally.

Set Time for Mental Exercises

Every day, provide your dog with mental exercises by maintaining rules, boundaries, and limitations. While meeting these needs, the affection you give to your dog will serve as a reward.

Always Get Ahead Of Your Dog

When leaving the house with your dog, always get ahead of your dog when going out of the door. This will show him who is in the leadership role.

As you guide him along the road or somewhere, make sure that he is not ahead of you or pulling you. Instead, keep him to your side or behind you. This is to demonstrate to your dog that you are the Alpha figure in the pack where he now belongs.

Let your Dog Earn His Treat

Command your dog to do something before giving him food, water, toys, or even affection. This is to show him that he needs to earn his treats. Even just a simple command of sitting or standing will do.

To sum it up, balance is the key to a harmonious relationship with your pet.

CHAPTER 2

Dog Training Basic Principles for Beginners

A well-trained dog is a pleasure to own, and training your dog is essentially asserting the rule of obedience. So it is vital that the training is not cruel. The training must enhance the relationship between you and your dog as it enriches the bond you are trying to create between the two of you. If your dog is well-trained, you can trust him to respond quickly and reliably to your every command.

During the training, you will learn to connect with each other through a special kind of language. Training takes a lot of practice and constant practice makes perfect. The more time you invest in training your dog, the more rewards you will get out of it. If you want your new puppy to be trained by a professional trainer, there are lots of them out there whom you can hire. However, a dog's loyalty is embedded on the one who started the training. Another option you have is signing up for a training class.

In the class, your puppy will learn the basic commands such as sit, stay, down, and come. He will also learn to walk nicely on a leash.

Training your dog involves giving him the command with a little piece of a treat as a reward. However, an effective training involves interpreting the dog's language and learning to communicate with him. This includes anticipating his responses and providing proper timing for giving rewards as well as corrections to inspire obedience.

Obedience Training: How to Get Started

As soon as you bring home a puppy, start training him. You can begin teaching him a few manners. A puppy has a short attention span so limit your training to about 10-15 minutes per session. You can repeat this many times every day until your puppy is able to master it.

In training, keep a bag of goodies handy. Every time your puppy does a good job, reward him with a treat. Rewards though may vary. You could give him a toy, pet him, or use verbal praises. Follow this up with praises such "Good boy!" This will motivate and instill in him the importance of obeying your command.

Avoid giving him treats in between training sessions just to please him. If he gets treats without having to earn them, he will not put much effort into his training. If your dog does not want to follow you, do not get mad and yell at him. Just withhold your reward. This will convey to him the message that he can't have it without his obedience.

One Word Is Enough

Saying your cue once is enough. Remember that a dog listening skill is sharp and he can always hear you the first time, and they are smart, too. Repeating the cue word a number of times will cause him to tune you out just as teenagers often do.

Schedule Training before Meals

Dogs are more attentive to commands if they are hungry. They know that their obedience can earn them a good bite of the tasty reward.

Don't Get Distracted When You're Training

You need to devote your full time to your dog during training. To avoid distractions, turn off your cell phone and ignore doorbells. In your first few sessions, you can do it inside a vacant room, large enough to accommodate your dog's movements. When your dog is able to obey a few basic commands, you can bring him outside in a fenced area. If unfenced, always keep him on a leash.

Provide your puppy with a positive environment during the training sessions. Even if you are upset with your puppy, do not yell at him. Dogs can easily get discouraged and nervous and will automatically stop paying attention to you when they are being yelled at.

Basic Dog Obedience Training

Here are some of the basic commands you can apply while training your puppy.

How to Sit

The "sit" command is the basic of all the basics. Once your puppy learns to follow this command, it will be easier to manage him until the time when he learns more self-control.

- Get on to your puppy's level and hold a treat close to his nose.
- As his head follows the treat, move your hand upward. When his head follows the movement of your hand, his butt will settle on the floor. When he manages to sit on his butt, give him the treat and praise him for a job well done. Repeat this lesson as many times as necessary until he manages to master the act.

- Never hold your treat too high, or else your puppy will jump for it. Hold it with your hand closed and high enough for him to extend his neck to reach out for it. Every time his butt hits the floor, say "Good sit!"

How to Come

- Try clipping a light line on your dog's collar and let him drag it.
- Pick up the line and follow him around. This will make him understand that the two of you are somehow connected.
- Then walk backward to encourage him to follow you this time. When he responds, give him a treat and say "yes!" Praise him and do it again, this time using the command "come!"
- Don't get into a habit of repeating the word several times if the dog fails to respond. Don't forget to apply the one-word, one-command rule.
- Never call your dog to come when you discipline him or he will associate it with a negative consequence.

How to Stay

- Put a leash on the dog.
- Have him sit comfortably beside you.
- Flatten your palm toward his muzzle and say "stay!"
- Step in front of him and then step back beside him.

As he stays where he is, reward him. If he moves, say "Oops" or "Uh-uh" and put him back to where he should be. Again, repeat the command with the hand signal. Repeat this many times in different locations. After rewarding him, say "okay" to break the command and release him from the "stay."

CHAPTER 3

Know Your Dogs Personality: A Basic Key for Success in Training

Dogs, like people, have varied personalities. Some are more active than others are while some are very smart. If you want to have better success training your dog, then you must tailor your approach to your dog's personality.

Dogs have different learning styles but like all pack animals, they are all looking for the gentle, benevolent type of leadership. A more violent and vicious type of training is never an effective approach to dog training as it can create behavioral problems or amplify an existing one.

When some dogs are easy to identify regarding personality types, other dogs might fall into several behavioral categories.

While hoping to achieve success in your dog training, you must learn the following categories of dog behavioral patterns.

Highly Sensitive

This type of dog is smart and quickly adapt to their environment. However, they are highly strung and easily shut down when exposed to a forceful behavior. Dogs belonging to this category need a subtle and tranquil mode of teaching.

Training Strategy

Because of their sensitivity, a gentle touch works better than a loud voice that can cause him to run away. Dogs belonging to this category are trainable and easy to handle. However, you must also bear in mind that any violent, vicious, and harsh treatment can damage these creatures and can make them fearful, shy, and very nervous. Breeds that fit into this category are Border Collies, German Shepherds, Australian Shepherds, most Toy breeds and some Pit Bull Terriers.

Happy-go-lucky

These are the thick-skinned bouncy types who are constantly on the go. They are easy going, hyperactive and can easily shift from a rough situation to normalcy without holding it against anyone. They are perfect for a busy, active household. All the same, they need gentle and sensitive directions just as others dogs do.

Training Strategy

You need to be obvious and straightforward in dealing with this kind. One-word rule does not apply to them as you definitely need to repeat yourself in the course of training these dogs. You also need to regularly set and enforce boundaries to let them fully understand every rule. Due to their hyperactive nature, it's hard for these dogs to switch from their rowdy and unruly behavior to being quiet. They are also easily distracted and can get caught up with what is going around them instead of focusing on what you are telling them. Examples of this type are the Bernese Mountain Dogs, Labradors, and Golden Retrievers.

Creative Thinkers

More so than other dogs, this type needs consistency and firmness in their training method. You will find out that these dogs have an entirely different mentality and point of view than you have about what is acceptable or is not acceptable. It's not really that that they're challenging your leadership. It is just that if you fail to give them clear guidance and communication, they are most likely to set their own rules and ignore yours.

Training Strategy

While training them as a leader of the pack, you need to be firm but low-toned in calling them. Be consistent and always enforce house rules and command. You can never afford to get lax in training these dogs or give a cold shoulder treatment when they neglect your orders. Constantly ask them to do something like, sit, lie down, or come before giving them a meal, a walk, or anything they want. Remember with this personality type, obedience must always be reinforced or they can take advantage of you. However, treating them with harshness and violence can make them aggressive and hostile to humans. Typically in this category are the alpha dogs.

In assessing your dog's category, rely more on their behavior and not on their breed as each has his own distinct personality just as humans do.

Tips for Training your Pet Boxer

Boxers are one of the most popular breeds of dog in the USA. Among dogs, Boxers are known to be smart, alert, and trustworthy. This is why they are considered formidable guard dogs, police and military occasionally will use them in their operations. They are used as service and therapy dogs, as well as guide dogs for the blind. In spite of their menacing looks, they have interesting traits that make them a family favorite.

Top Eight Tips for a Boxer Training Success

TIP #1:

This breed has a distinct trait and you must be aware of it. Ideally, training for a Boxer pup must start when he turns 3 weeks old. It is during this period when he will learn to obey simple commands. Boxers are loving and faithful to their masters and family but distrustful of strangers. They are also smart and friendly but fierce and determined when aroused. These animals are cheerful companions even in their old age. However, watch out for factors that ignite their unpleasant behavior lest it becomes a part of their personality.

TIP #2:

Socialization is important for a boxer. Boxers in general, love to play and interact with human beings. If trained properly, a Boxer will grow to be responsible. This dog is far from being the loner type. Without enough socialization, your Boxer's temperament will arise and his frustration will cause you trouble.

TIP #3:

Regular exercise is vital since this animal is quite active. His training must include sport and outdoor training. This will keep him active and agile as well as help him manage his energy level while indoors. The exercise can be walking and playing sports like ball-tossing or Frisbee. A Boxer enjoys running free in the open and playing for hours. More exercise means more strength and vigor for him

TIP #4:

As his leader, you must assume the role of an alpha dog. It is imperative that he treats you as a master to have full control over him. As a leader, be strict and dominant especially with the rules. Overpower him and never let him overtake you in any way. Adhere to a strict regiment until he learns and fully understands what behavior is acceptable and required especially when you let him go outdoors for a walk or to exercise.

TIP #5:

Never forget to reward your dog every time he follows the rules. Positive reinforcement is important in dealing with him especially during his training. You may give him treats for being good and never fail to praise him when he has done something worth appreciating. Just as important as the reward, correct him when he is wrong. However, refrain from giving harsh punishment. This may trigger aggression. Discipline must come in a firm but cool manner.

TIP #6:

Spend time with your Boxer even beyond training hours. This will strengthen your bond. Keeping him company will elevate your relationship to the next level. Never let your dog feel he is unwanted or neglected.

TIP #7:

Teach your dog tricks. It is important that you provide him skills. A trick or two can harness your dog's mental development besides impressing your friends and family. Skills like rolling, kneeling, crawling are just examples of basic tricks you may teach your dog. These tricks will turn him into a very clever friend.

TIP #8:

The greatest training tip that will assure your training success is to approach your dog with patience, persistence and a great amount of love. Remember that dogs are sensitive and can fully sense emotions you have towards them. Most often than not, your pet can read you clearly.

II – Phase Two

Application Methods for Success

CHAPTER 4

Essential Housebreaking Basic Techniques

House breaking a puppy can be a stressful activity but it need not be.

Your Dog's Physical Condition

Your dog's health will surely have an effect on his aptitude in training. Therefore, make sure that right after you bring him home, you have him checked by a veterinarian. If your doggie has a bladder infection, cystitis, or even parasites, he must be treated first. Your dog needs a general check up by a veterinarian which will include fecal tests and deworming. If you skip this important step, your dog could bring a parasite into your home and infect everyone, it's a good guess that you don't want to get worms from your new doggie!

Quality Food for Your Dog

Feeding your puppy with a quality food is also essential. A steady diet of high-quality is advisable and if possible, avoid changing brands when it's not necessary. If for some reason you need to change his food, do it gradually over a period of 4-7 days by mixing both brands, lessening the amount of the old one until you can totally eliminate it for the new one.

Potty Training for Your Dog

Being a part of your family, your dog is sure to be spending some time inside the house, so be sure to teach him where it is ok for him to relieve himself. It is not much fun to have a puppy wandering around the house making a mess everywhere he goes. Your puppy needs to be trained to go potty outside where you tell him to go. Potty training can take a lot of time and energy, but it is absolutely a necessity.

When your puppy is not confined to a small area, he needs close supervision. Young dogs still don't have enough control of bladder and they usually have to potty frequently. To avoid spending most of your time and effort cleaning up your puppys accidents, watch out for signs such as circling, sniffing the floor, or suddenly running out of your sight.

Potty training is often a trial of stress for everyone in the house and this includes you since you are his master. However, be patient and use the proper techniques. Always start training your puppy his toiletry ethics while young starting the very first day you bring him home. During his early years, he doesn't have much bowel and bladder control but if you start later, it could be more difficult.

When you begin your training, confine your pet to a small area restricting his movements, either in a single room, a crate or a tethered leash. Teach your pup the idea that he needs to conduct his business outside the area of restriction. Your puppy is sensitive to the smell. Observe that your pup will constantly go back to the same spot where he had previously relieved himself. To keep him from returning to the place, be sure to clean it up and remove the odor. Try neutralizing soiled areas such as carpet or any ground surface with a pet odor netralizer such as Mature's Miracle, Fresh N Clean or Outright Pet Odor Eliminator. As your dog starts to recognize what's expected of him, try expanding the area until he is able to master the habit.

When left alone in the house, crate training is highly recommended to secure a puppy or adolescent dog. Crate training must be introduced properly to prevent accidents and keep your dog safe when you're not around to watch him closely. Avoid using a crate for a long period and never use the crate as a punishment. It's fine to bring your dog outside of his crate from time to time.

Take note, however, that crate training and any other confinement method should be done in balance with enough exercise and socialization. Interactive playtime and daily companionship are important to dogs. Excessive periods of isolation are detrimental and may lead to various problems in behavior like destructive behavior, self-mutilation, hyperactivity, and too much barking or whining.

Know Your Puppy's signals

You must keep a journal of your dog's elimination activities for a few days to determine when he needs to go potty. Figure out how long after eating or drinking anything it takes for him to show signs that he needs to go potty. Subtract 15 to 30 minutes and that is your dog's Safety Zone. The safety zone is the temporary length of time when your puppy can control his urine.

All dogs have to "take a break" shortly after eating, drinking water, playing, sleeping or chewing. For a puppy more than 10 weeks old, that means urinating between 5-10x a day. A dog 6-11 months of age needs 5-6 walks a day, while an adult dog needs 3-4 walks a day, and an elderly dog needs at least 3-4 walks daily.

For dogs that are confined during the night, take him for a walk outside early in the morning before he soils indoors. The duration could be dependent on how long your pet will go before he needs to relieve himself. When your puppy had relieved himself, in the correct place, praise him or give him a treat.

Early Interaction with People

It is important for your dog to be introduced to calm and friendly people especially children as this will help form his social behavior around people. The earlier your puppy get used to visitors in the house, the more he becomes comfortable around them. This will help eliminate cases of a dog biting accident in the future. Likewise, bring your puppy to public places, so he can be exposed to loud noises, crowded areas, and traffic. Just make sure, he won't be anywhere around any other dogs.

Familiarize your dog with command words so that he can understand what you want him to do such as "potty" or "bombs away." After he is done with his business, provide him with a treat as a reward and future incentive to show your pet that you're pleased with his behavior. Delay in giving praise or reward is not effectual, so observe him as he goes to the right spot when doing his business. It is not advisable to give a bowl of drinking water to your puppy after 9 p.m. unless the weather is exceedingly hot.

CHAPTER 5 –

Easy Methods to Stop Your Dog from Irritating Chewing Habits

One thing that most people cannot cope with about puppies is their chewing habits. How irritating it can be when you find out that your shoes, the cushion, and your slippers have been chewed into pieces. However, before you finally go amuck and send your puppy back to where you got him, understand why he behaves like that. While your puppy needs the right housebreaking rules from you, then it is essential that you as the master, needs to be trained as well.

Like little kids, it's natural for puppies to chew on anything all the time. Therefore your dog training must take into account these natural tendencies. They want to chew because they are teething, anxious or bored. Understanding this, you need to look for ways that can distract them from chewing before this can become a habit.

The first time you see your puppy playfully bite on something, do not ignore, or tolerate them. This is a sign that something is wrong with them. Though we can say this is natural in them, we can also check and correct this inherent tendency so you do not need to put up with that bad chewing habit. Instantly point out to your pet that what he is doing is not allowed, but provide an alternative activity to distract him. You may give him a toy bone instead or anything he can chew. Avoid giving him something that can resemble things you don't want his teeth on like stuff toys, shoes or something soft.

In rectifying your puppy's behavior, avoid shouting or any giving any physical punishment. This will only confuse him without him understanding what he did wrong. Try using the following instead:

1. To divert your puppy's attention as it begins chewing on anything he can find, present him with a dog bone and praise him when he starts chewing it. This is to show him that what he is doing is acceptable.

2. Keep your puppy from getting bored. When you can't stop your puppy the first time he chews something he shouldn't, it could go on forever as a habit. Even after his teething stage, he will keep on chewing on anything he wants. To keep your puppy from getting bored, plan a regular dog training exercise with them. Play with your puppy as often as you can. This will keep them from doing anything harmful aside from enjoying the fun. You will be surprise to see how much you will enjoy it yourself.

3. Most often, it's when you're out of the house or at night when you're separated from your puppy that these chewing activities occur. It's because you're puppy could be suffering from anxiety. To keep him from this, use a bitter-tasting Cayenne pepper spray before he can totally ruin your belongings. Spray them on the object he wants to chew. This can make him connect such objects with a bad taste.

4. When you're not with your puppy, try the crate training. Limit his access to your house area and instead confine him to a single space which he can call his own.

5. Consistency in training is vital. To successfully get your dog out of his chewing before it can become a full-grown habit; make sure that your actions are consistent. Prepare rules yourself and see to it that your puppy is following them. With proper training, chewing will never be a problem with your puppy.

While the above rules can rectify your dog's chewing behavior, you may as well rectify yours. If he needs training, so do you! As your dog's master, you have to be consistent and smart in dealing with him. Here are some things you need to think about.

To start, get your things away from your pet like gloves, shoes, racket, slippers, hat or anything which you think can attract him to chew on. If he can't see anything on the ground or floor to chew, how can he do it? You, therefore, have control over him by simply outsmarting him.

When he is destructive when you are not home, then either crate him or arrange for someone to play with him or take him for a walk outside when you are not there to do it yourself. Dogs are hyperactive, therefore, provide him with an activity that can get rid of that extra energy.

Lastly, to reiterate some basic instruction, when you find your dog chewing on your favorite shoe, avoid getting mad. Just interrupt him from this harmful activity and check on his bad behavior. Take the shoe out of his mouth and say "NO!" firmly. Replace it with a chewable bone toy. Remember this: Do not use his name. It is important that you use his name in praising him and not when reprimanding him.

CHAPTER 6 –

Teaching Your Dog Four Basic Commands

When you bring a puppy home, he becomes a part of the family and therefore needs to conform to the basic house rules. By nature, a dog wants to please its master as they naturally belong to a pack in the wilds. However, like a new baby in your household, he can only master the art of conforming to habits as you guide him in his formative years.

It is therefore, dependent in the way you train him that he will learn to conform to every house rule.

There are some essential basics that you need to teach your dog. A dog's life does not only revolve around tricks and treats. He needs to be loyal to the family and obedience is part of your goal while training him.

Obedience Training

Obedience is basic in every dog's training. While it's a pleasure to be hanging with your pet, he could be also a great nuisance if not properly trained. A disobedient dog is nothing but a real pain in the neck!!

You can later treat your dog to the higher level of training but remember that the foundation of your dog's character is always dependent on his basic training. So be sure that you train him efficiently for your future success!

Sit - This needs to be the basic of all the basics. This act depicts obedience and peace while being attentive to what you can teach him next. A dog that sits, has its focus on you as its trainer, so grab this opportunity the very first time you take a hold on him.

Stay – this further gives your dog a place for his own calmness and serenity. As he becomes still in one place, he can have his utter silence and relaxation. Though you can trust your dog to be attentive to what's going on around him, even while he is in this position.

Heel – This teaches your dog to be submissive teaching him that you're always in command. Keeping your dog at heel teaches him not to surpass your authority while remaining close to you. Animals are sensitive creatures. They can have a way of giving a certain level of understanding beyond the physical aspect as you grow to develop that special bond.

Come - As soon as your puppy begins to recognize the name you have given him, teach him this act for a quick response to your commands. Dogs love to please you and when they hear, they know that it's time that you have your focus on him. The "come" command leads to the expectation of bonding and rewards for your dog.

In teaching your dog the basic training commands, it is highly recommended to use the reinforcement method.

A positive reinforcement prefers giving rewards for a good behavior rather than inflicting punishment for unwanted behavior. This kind of training gives your dog an exciting and enjoyable experience while under training and therefore strengthens the bond between the two of you.

Lastly, while training your dog, don't forget other members of your family. It is essential that there is consistency in your training. Make everyone aware of what you are doing to avoid distraction and disturbance in your dog's formative period.

CHAPTER 7

How to Get Your Dog to Stop Barking

It could be irritating when a dog barks too much. We are expecting our dog to bark only when there are burglars or intruders in the house. However, if your dog seems to enjoy barking too often, then you need to give him proper training. This training is essential to give you peace of mind and to let your dog know that this is not an acceptable behavior. Too much barking from your dog can also disturb your neighbors. With proper training, your dog will know when or when not to bark.

A dog barks when he wants your attention. So when your dog barks, attend immediately to his needs. Do not neglect when you hear your dog is barking. Most of the time, your dog barks needs immediate attention. When you see that your dog is barking without any reason, you splash some water on his face and leave him without saying anything. This will tell him that you do not approve his behavior. Making him realize that this behavior does not impress you will stop him from doing so.

You can also divert your dog's attention when you give him some toys to play with. Remember that dogs are loyal to their master so they want to attract your attention most of the time. So never fail to give your dog enough attention and reward him every time he has done something impressive. This will help him learn what to do to earn your praise.

Dogs can bark too much when he cannot see you or when you leave the house. Train your dog to be independent. It is better to crate train you dog every time you are not around. He will feel safe inside the house even when he cannot see you around. Make sure that you have left him enough food, water, and proper ventilation. A dog can bark loudly when they are hungry, thirsty or want to go for a walk.

If the dog training is done properly, your dog will not bark anymore unless something really is needed. Trained dogs also do not feel any discomfort even when left alone inside the house as long as he is well provided. A dog when properly taken care of can behave properly like humans.

III – Phase Three

Love and Consistency over Time

CHAPTER 8 –

Love and Discipline the Key Combinations for Successful Obedience Training

As emphasized at the beginning chapters, once you bring a puppy or dog home, he automatically becomes a part of your family. He becomes just like your child and therefore should be loved and disciplined as well.

Bear in mind that you are his master and parent at the same time. Training him is one of the best and loving acts you can do for him. It also serves as line of communication between you and your dog or pup. There are a lot of reasons why you should train him, but the three main reasons may be summarized as these: 1) for his social standing; 2) for his mental workout; and 3) for his safety.

Train Your Dog to Help Him Boost His Social Standing

Let's talk about the number one reason first—that is to boost his social standing. You have to remember that dogs are social animals that will still behave as animals without proper training. They can chew on furniture; pee and poop inside your room; or bark and howl all night. The trick here is to help your dog transfer his natural behavior to outlets that are suitable in the domestic setting.

His behavior would say a lot about him. A well-trained canine will be more than welcomed in any home. Do you remember some instances when you silently noted a child's behavior in your kid's birthday party? You might have subconsciously (or consciously) inscribed those who would be of good influence to your kid, and those who wouldn't make it to the list on his next birthday party. This might just be true for your furry buddy. If he is stubborn, chances are he won't be too welcomed in other homes.

Train Your Dog for His Mental Workout

Second reason—and arguably the most important reason—is for his mental workout. As it is, dogs are not only social animals but are cognitive and emotional beings, too. Now, who doesn't want a smart and intelligent dog? It is important for you to understand that your dog's cognitive exercises are as important as his daily physical exercises. This will keep him from boredom and from his destructive behavior.

There are two kinds of cognitive exercises that you can give your dog. The first one is the "basic mental exercises." You don't have to hire a professional trainer just to give your dog these simple exercises. You can give them yourself and while you at it, consider your training time as your bonding time with him. The other one is the "complex mental exercises." No, this does not even require the help of a professional trainer either, but you might as well invest your time to give him this kind of training. Complex mental exercises demand intense involvement and in some cases, may involve formal training.

Basic Mental Exercises

If you're thinking that these simple tasks include teaching your dog how to sit, come or stay, then you're right. However, fun activities like a game of fetch serve as a mental exercise as well. The game requires your dog's focus and attention, and these two are already mental tasks. Any activity that implores your dog's attention is considered a mental exercise, and such activities are sufficient to help your dog boost his psychological health.

Another one is a game that requires the help of Kong toys. This kind of game will help your dog think about his strategy on how to get to the biscuits you put inside the toy. Notice that your dog doesn't have to be physically active in this activity, but he can exercise his cognitive abilities and keep him from getting bored.

Complex Mental Exercises

As mentioned earlier, complex mental exercises implore a rather concentrated involvement. It makes sense to play games with your dog first for the warm up. Through playing games, he will learn how to follow rules; and following rules is another great form of mental exercise.

Hide and seek is a popular bonding game for families. You can include your dog when you and your family play this game. As you know, dogs are generally good in tracking and retrieving simply because they just want to be with their owners. This particular game then requires your dog to use his cognitive skills in order to trace you.

You get the idea of the fetching game for the simple mental exercises. Let's bring it to another level. This time, you will be the one to retrieve an item from your dog. The objective is to help your dog learn strategies that will help him keep the item away from your grasp, you will see, your dog will first try to avoid and dodge your attempts to take the item away from you. Later, you can observe that his strategies are evolving as he learns ways to keep his goals.

Meanwhile, the most complex set of cognitive exercises can be found in a formal training. We are talking about training your dog to obey commands, learn tricks and even perform in dog competitions. During the training, your dog has the great potential to expand his mental capacities. These kinds of mental exercises may be tasking but these greatly give him (and you) the assurance that he will be safe wherever he goes. You may never anticipate it, but this kind of training might just save his life one day.

Obedience Training Should be Enjoyable and Rewarding

Learning and training are forms of discipline. Your dog follows rules and restrains some of his nature in order to achieve a specific goal. Just like we, humans, feel from time-to-time, such activities are tiresome. It is good to give your furry friend rewards every time he accomplishes something. Remember that you are forming a bond with your dog, and having said that, your obedience training must be fun and rewarding.

Keep your training sessions brief and pleasant. Refrain from prolonging your training as this will be dull, tedious and boring for your canine. As much as possible, make your obedience training a daily routine so your dog will not forget what he has learned. Most importantly, bear in mind that your obedience training is the same as your dog's favorite activities. Hence, your dog's favorite activities become his training ground.

When it comes to rewarding, remember to reward your dog for good behavior. The more times he receives rewards, the faster he learns. Thus, it is important that you create scenarios wherein your dog can practice performing the right thing. Don't forget to shower him with praises most especially during the times that he is behaving good-naturedly.

Issues of Reprove during the Obedience Training

Constantly reprimanding your dog in the form of yelling (i.e. "Bad dog!" "Get off!" "Stop that!" "No!") Can eventually become meaningless words and are disregarded. Now, if you praise your dog most of the time for his proper behavior, then your reproves will give more meaning. If the need to reprimand your dog arises, all you have to do is to immediately show him what you want him to do. Afterward, recognize his efforts and good behavior. For instance, you caught him pulling off the drapes. Just tell him, "Off!" and direct him to his toys right away. Once he settled down and munched on his toys, don't forget to praise him for his behavior.

Moreover, note that your reprove should be short, sharp and requires the sense of urgency. Refrain from nagging by all means. Do not hurt your dog for this type of punishment usually generates or worsens problems.

CHAPTER 9

Give Guidance and Be Your Dog's Best Friend

Nowadays, many adults tend to decide to try their "parenting" on dogs before they experience the real thing. That's being practical and there's quite a good logic there. Surprisingly, child parenting and dog parenting have their similarities. After all, they are both about responsibilities of rearing up someone.

The below section give you points in how to train your dog. The guidelines show how you can make obedience training much simpler and easier for both you and your best friend.

Be Consistent

This calls for regularity of commands at each given time. For instance, you teach your dog the command, "come." Use the word "come" for at least a week; "come here" for the following week; and "come here, buddy" for the next week. This way, you won't confuse him.

1. **Make It a Step-by-Step Training**

   Start with easy commands and simple exercises in a familiar setting void of distractions. This could be your backyard wherein your dog won't be able to meet any other dogs. Once your dog achieves consistency, proceed to what professional trainers dub as the 3 D's—distance, duration and distractions. For example, for distance, you can start by standing one meter away from your dog, then two meters away. For duration, you can ask for a three-count stay, then five-count stay the next. For distractions, you can add a moving toy, some scattered treats, or another dog (or person). Just make sure that your furry buddy has mastered the current challenge before you move on to the next level. If he wasn't able to get the challenge, try it again next time but make the pace slower in order for him to catch up.

2. **Do not Repeat Commands**

   Make him respond to your first command. Repeating it makes your dog think that he doesn't need to respond to your first command at once.

3. **Do not Lose Your Cool**

   Patience is a must when it comes to training your dog. Do not hurt him through your words or actions. Bawling, spanking or yanking your dog by the leash will not give him a proper and healthy training. It will just teach him that you are someone to be afraid of, instead someone he can trust. If you feel that you're losing patience, simply end the session and continue it later. Remember that you can earn your dog's respect and trust by being calm, consistent and fair.

4. **Give Treats and Rewards**

One of the most effective ways to lure and reward your dog is to give
him food treats. However, if your dog is not fond of food, try to give
him alternatives such as his favorite toy, affectionate gestures (such as a
good rubbing on his tummy or scratching on behind his ears) or verbal
praises.

5. Give Rewards Periodically

Once your dog masters a command, give him special rewards for his
best performance. Plan how you can give rewards and treats. For
instance, you can sometimes pat his head whenever he makes a good
performance and for his best, you can let him get a food treat.

6. Observe Proper Timing

Be sure to give your praise or reward right after when he achieves
something. Do not let one good performance go unnoticed.

7. Keep Your Training Brief and Pleasant

Maintain a positive mood instead of a serious one. Remember that fun
and enjoyment are key factors that greatly affect the product of your
training. Moreover, make your training sessions short. You can start
with five to ten minutes and you can make several mini sessions
throughout the day.

8. Introduce Your Dog to the Members of Your Family and in Various Settings

If you want your dog to obey the other members of your family, then let
him practice with them. To make him obedient in different locations or
settings, then practice him in those places.

9. Always Practice

Even if your dog has learned something, it doesn't mean that he has
learned it for life. Know that he can lose those skills if you don't

practice them on a regular basis. Thus, keep in mind to practice all of those tricks and skills frequently. Giving your dog proper training is one of the best gifts he can ever receive. It benefits him in different ways and also strengthens the bonds you both share together.

In addition to the basic guidelines, you can also get more ideas from this list of Do's and Don'ts to forge a much stronger bond with your best friend.

Do's and Don'ts

Do be consistent with your words, actions and expectations with your dog. Do not frustrate your dog with your unrealistic expectations.

Do regularly train your dog in order to physically and mentally stimulate him. Do not let him stagnate for he will soon deteriorate if you let him.

Do observe enjoyment and fun while training him. Do not be too serious or boring during your training time.

Do be pleasant and kind whenever your dog comes to you despite his misdemeanors. Do not do anything he considers unpleasant when he comes to you.

Do remember that your dog is a social animal; hence, make some time to get your dog hang out with other dogs and people. Do not isolate him from them, particularly from your family.

Do use a normal voice tone each time you give a command as your dogs' hearing ability is very acute. Do not yell or shout at him as he is not deaf and your act does not actually enhance his understanding.

Do use your dog's name whenever you want to get his attention and tell him what you want him to do. Do not call him by his name and expect him to read your mind.

Do constantly reward him with treats, affection, and verbal praises. Don't lock him up or put him out whenever he fails to obey a command or perform a trick. Do not reward disagreeable behaviors.

CHAPTER 10

Obedience Training Takes Time Even Though Some Success May Come Easily

We learn that most things in life are not acquired easily. It is also true when it comes to training your beloved canine. Understand that obedience training requires time and a lot of patience. You need to observe a step-by-step method, and even have to do a back step should it be deemed necessary. And even before that, you have to understand a few points about your dog.

Know that the first year is the hardest year for both you and your dog. This is also the best time to start the obedience training and teach your dog a few tricks. Dogs in general are very active creatures and they want a very busy lifestyle.

Your dog is ready to learn from your on the very first day you acquire him. To start forming your special bond, you can take him for a lot of walks, play games and spend as much time as you have with him.

As your dog grows up and gets to know you more, teach him who is in-charge and who is the rule-setter. This is the most crucial part of your obedience training and is never an easy endeavor. If your dog doesn't recognize who is the boss, this can create problems. He will definitely follow his own rules, which completely go against your domestic rules.

Furthermore, you have to understand about your dog's personality and character. We can't deny that it's important for your beloved canine to understand you since you're the one who is in charge of him. Nevertheless, you also have the obligation to know about him. To help you with, here are some points in how to read your dog's body language:

Your Dog's Body Language

In general, dogs have always communicated using body language. This includes body postures, noises, scents and facial expressions. They use their mouth, ears, eyes and tail to show their emotions. As an owner, you have to learn how to interpret your dog's body language in order to understand his intentions.

Tail

You can easily interpret the mood of your furry friend through his tail. A wagging tail is usually interpreted as a sign of pleasure and interest.

Most dogs hold their tails 45 degrees to the back. While this may vary from breed to breed, but this tail stance can be interpreted as "interest" and "alertness." Meanwhile, if your dog's tail waved slowly and rather stiffly, it may mean that he is angry. If it is drooped, it means that he is nervous or anxious. And if it is lowered over his hindquarters, it means that he is afraid.

Eyes

You will know if your dog feels pleasure when his eyes are half-closed. However, if his eyes are wide open, it may indicate aggression.

Smile

Some breeds like the Labradors, open their mouths in what they call a "lop-sided grin" as a sign of friendliness. This is also true to some submissive dogs. But when his lips are drawn back and he bares his teeth, then it is certainly aggression.

Understanding Your Dog's Attitude

Whining

Your dog may whine and whimper to gain your approval if he has made a mistake. You will be making a big mistake if you comfort him during this episode. It will make him think that you are actually praising him for doing his misdeed. On the other hand, if you ignore him and only praise him after he stops whining, this will help him think otherwise.

Barking

While barking is a totally in nature of a dog's behavior, know that it should always be in control. Teach him to stop barking when he is told to stop. You can start training him by letting him bark two or three times. Praise him for this and then say, "Stop barking." Hold out your food treat in front of him. This should give him a cue to stop since he will sniff it according to his instinct. After a few moments of staying silent, give him his reward. You can gradually add time in the process, but make sure that you also vary your rewards.

Meanwhile, if your dog exhibits excessive barking that you cannot control, seek advice from a veterinarian. He should be able to advice you of the next steps that may involve therapy or a specialist training.

How Your Dog Reads You

More often than not, your dog chooses to read you through your body language and signals. He immediately knows how you feel even without listening to you. Therefore, if you want your communication with your dog to progress, improve your body language.

How Your Dog Learns

Dogs usually learn by association; hence, if he does something good, give him a reward. You must understand that the reward must be in connection with his action. Additionally, you must reward him right after he accomplishes something.

He must understand and learn the things that he can and cannot do. You must identify his potentially dangerous behaviors and handle them as soon as possible. Learn to say a sharp "no" to rebuke him, but make sure that you redirect him to another positive activity. Never shout or hit him if you want your dog to have a healthy learning approach.